BEYOND KNOCHE'S LAW

BEYOND KNOCHE'S LAW

KEITH KNOCHE

Pacific Press Publishing Association
Mountain View, California
Oshawa, Ontario

Cover and inside art by Keith Knoche

Copyright 1983 by
Pacific Press Publishing Association
Printed in United States of America

Library of Congress Cataloging in Publication Data

Knoche, Keith.
  Beyond Knoche's law.

  (Redwood)
1. Christian life—Anecdotes, facetiae, satire, etc. I.
Title.
BV4905.2.K58   1983   248.4'0207   82-7876
ISBN 0-8163-0488-2   AACR2

DEDICATION

To my Grandma
. . . Gladys, whose hugs, homemade quilts, and apple pie are the best in the known world. And whose boysenberry jam makes you wish you were a slice of bread. With love.

Contents

Prologue

Throughout history, pundits and poseurs have regaled us with the laws of the universe, the subtle yet immutable substructure which is the basis of cosmic order. They have given us such unforgettable gems as "time is money," "you are what you eat," and "beauty is only skin deep." Have you ever wondered where these wise axioms came from? Neither have I.

But since writing *Knoche's Law* ("If something can go wrong, it will—but there's a lesson in it somewhere"), I have been literally besieged with a host of other principles, theorems, and corollaries. These have caused me to go deep into thought, to examine the substance of my inner self, the core of my being— my id, my libido, my ego, my alter-ego, my super-ego, my pancreas, and numerous other visceral organs.

By studying and applying these various cosmic laws, I have achieved greater selfhood. For as Freud so eloquently said, "A man without a self is like a fish without a bicycle." (Many of Freud's statements have yet to be proved or even understood.)

One thing is known: These universal mandates were forged out of common human experience—the day-to-day hassles which are the stuff of life.

For instance, has this ever happened to you? Have

9

you ever received a phone call the minute you jumped into the shower?

Has it ever started raining the day you washed your car? Or stopped raining when you bought an umbrella?

Have you ever, while using your blow dryer, had your hair catch fire?

Perhaps you realized at the time that something was afoot, that some great universal force was at work—a power beyond human reason and understanding. And yet, these very enigmas prompted the laws of which I speak. They came over a period of centuries and cover the whole spectrum of human experience.

From the men of religion (Moses, Hammurabi) we have received the Moral Laws.

From the artists (Michelangelo, Rembrandt, Da Vinci) we have gleaned the Laws of Aesthetics.

From the mystics (Buddha, Mohammed, Confucius, Cosmo Gupner), the Laws of Karma.

Without exception these great codes came as the result of difficulty and trial. They were born in the crucible of conflict and tempered in the sitzbath of adversity. Man learned through the things he suffered.

My dad once put it this way: "Good judgment is the result of experience . . . and experience is the result of bad judgment." Ah, here is a great truth! The chronicle of the past attests that this is verity, not balderdash!

The great lawgiver Hammurabi may have been burned a time or two by purchasing a "lemon" from "Honest Nahor's Used Chariot Emporium" before chiseling out his monumental code of ethics.

Do you suppose Michelangelo ever dropped paint in his eye while creating Adam on the ceiling of the Sistine Chapel? Imagine, screaming in church!

Or maybe it was on one of those dreary nights after the Monks' Convention, when Confucius had to wash

10

all the chopsticks by himself, that he quipped, "Many hands make light work."

Do you see what I'm getting at? By facing and mastering life's problems we mature and grow. This is often a painful process, but necessary for total development.

Think of your own experience. By confronting your greatest trials you realized your greatest triumphs. For in those moments of difficulty and despair you reached out for someone; you reached out for God.

It was no different for Jesus. He graduated summa cum laude from the School of Hard Knocks right there in "Iniquityville" (Nazareth), Palestine. The Bible says, "He learned obedience from the things which he suffered." Hebrews 5:8, NASB. Is it possible that the Son of God needed those tough experiences to make Him physically, mentally, and spiritually mature?

Fact: Life is brimful of difficulties, problems, and frustrations. But God can use our troubles to make us ready for His kingdom.

The Bible puts it this way: "Is your life full of difficulties and temptations? Then be happy, for when the way is rough, your patience has a chance to grow." "And patience develops strength of character in us and helps us trust God more each time we use it until finally our hope and faith are strong and steady." James 1:2, 3; Romans 5:4, LB.

So this trip I'm going to take you *Beyond Knoche's Law* into the wonderful world of theorems and postulates where faith can grow. If you pay attention, you may discover a great deal about yourself. And, what's more, you may discover a great deal about God and His amazing love for you.

Note: Names of certain people in some of the stories have been changed.

11

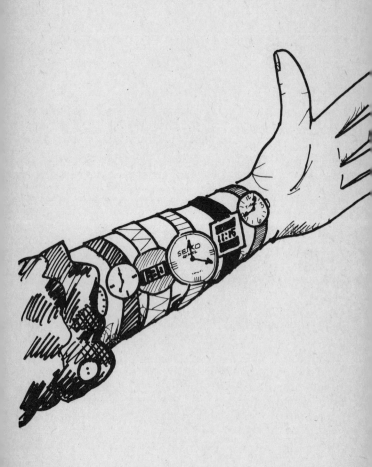

CHAPTER 1
SEGAL'S LAW:

A man with one watch knows what time it is. A man with two watches is never sure.

I'll never forget Dartmouth Narzel. When I lived in Honolulu a few years back, we met on several occasions. One thing is certain: If you ever met Dartmouth, you'd never forget him.

Now I don't want to cast any reflections on Dartmouth's lily-white character. He was a decent guy. But he had his peculiarities. Dartmouth was, shall we say, a dim bulb. He was a brick shy of a full load. On an IQ test he would peak out at about 87!

People didn't make fun of Dartmouth, even though he wore a gray wool overcoat in the stifling summer heat and rode a slightly bent '49 Schwinn Silver Streak. They felt sorry for him. So did I.

One sunny July day down at Ala Moana Beach, I saw Dartmouth pedaling along on his bike. I flagged him down and we chatted, mostly about the fact that his brother Ernest (IQ 84) had just saved up enough money to buy something he had always wanted—a monogrammed set of corduroy forks. Then I made the fatal mistake of asking Dartmouth for the time.

He obliged by pulling up his overcoat sleeve to reveal no less than eight (count them) wristwatches—a Waltham, two Bulovas, three Timexes, a Spiro Agnew, and a Mickey Mouse.

Dartmouth spent the next ten minutes trying to determine if it was, in fact, 11:15, 10:46, 3:45, 1:12, 7:37, 9:10, and—well, one of Mickey's hands was broken off, but Dartmouth didn't know whether it was Mickey's hour or minute hand.

Dartmouth never did, as it turned out, figure out what time it was. Frustration. So he climbed on his slightly warped Silver Streak and tooled off down the street, leaving me totally confused. What time was it?

Moments later, I asked a Japanese tourist the time and was immediately informed that it was precisely 2:30 p.m., according to his Seiko. There was no confusion, but then he had only one watch!

Here is proof positive of the truth of Segal's Law: "A man with one watch knows what time it is. A man with two watches is never sure." And we might add this corollary: "A man with eight watches is totally exasperated!"

Jesus put the same idea in different words when He commented, "You cannot serve two masters: God and money. For you will hate one and love the other, or else the other way around." Matthew 6:24, LB.

Now obviously, Jesus wasn't talking about wristwatches. But the principle applies nonetheless. Jesus was speaking of the whole arena of conflict in the battle between good and evil. He was talking about the spiritual warfare that rages within the human heart and mind.

You see, the great controversy is not being waged by angels in the distant reaches of space. It is being waged between your own two ears. The real battle is for your mind—your will.

Religionists and psychologists have long agreed that the will is the true command center of man. Whoever controls the will, controls the mind, the heart, the life.

Who controls your will? Who is in charge of your mind? Whom do you serve?

The issue is complicated by the fact that there are opposing forces at work to control the will. There is within every human personality a good nature and an evil nature. The apostle Paul refers to them as the spiritual nature and the carnal nature.

Sigmund Freud recognized the active conflict that occurs in a man's mind because of the presence of these two different forces. In fact, the Freudian school of psychoanalysis believes that this cerebral conflict is the source of most of man's psychic disorders.

Carl Jung, the founder of the school of analytical psychology, was also impressed by the fact that neuroses were caused by the battle between two warring cerebral agents: "What drives people to war with themselves is the intuition or the knowledge that they consist of two persons in opposition to one another. The conflict may be between the sensual and the spiritual man. It is what Faust means when he says, 'Two souls, alas, dwell in my breast.' "

Robert Louis Stevenson, in *Dr. Jekyl and Mr. Hyde*, gave a fascinating description of an individual who was swayed one moment by the beneficent Dr. Jekyl in his nature, and then the next minute he was turned into and controlled by his evil and murderous Mr. Hyde nature.

With a little introspection, each of us can sense the presence of two opposite forces within. It is especially easy to sense our duality when we have a moral issue to decide. It is not pleasant to have two pugilists battling it out and raising a rumpus in our cerebral attics.

An old Indian lived deep in the woods of northern Canada. Every so often he would make a trek eighteen miles to the trading post to purchase supplies. This particular trip, as the trader was loading the goods—salt, flour, beans—on the Indian's dogsled, he inadvertently dropped four pennies down in the supply box. Not knowing this, the old Indian headed back to his cabin.

The very next day, here came the Indian traveling those eighteen long miles back to the trading post. Opening his fist he displayed the four shiny coins, explaining that the trader had dropped these in his pack by mistake.

"What!" exclaimed the trader. "You came back all that way to return four pennies!"

"You see," said the Indian slowly in broken English, "me get good Indian and bad Indian in heart. Good Indian say, 'Take 'em back.' Bad Indian say, 'Keep 'em.' Good Indian and bad Indian argue and fight all night long. Keep me awake. So I bring 'em back."

This simple story expresses a great truth. For we have all heard these opposing "voices" within us. These are nothing more than the two natures struggling for supremacy. And as uncomplimentary as it sounds, we often find it a real battle to determine which of these two natures will rule us. But sooner or later one will win out. For no one can serve two masters. Furthermore, the person who tries to serve two masters is frustrated and miserable. Look at poor Dartmouth!

For this purpose God has given us His Spirit. And the person who yields to this Heavenly Force is under divine control. "Now if Christ does live within you his presence means that your sinful nature is dead." "We are living no longer by the dictates of our sinful nature, but in obedience to the promptings of the Spirit." Romans 8:10, Phillips.

"But now you must yourselves lay aside all anger, passion, malice, cursing, filthy talk—have done with

16

them! Stop lying to one another, now that you have discarded the old nature with its deeds and have put on the new nature, which is being constantly renewed in the image of its Creator and brought to know God.'' Colossians 3:8-10, NEB.

Surrendering one's will to the divine will may seem to be a negative procedure, but it gives positive dividends. Only by allowing Christ's Force to control the heart and mind can we experience real living, new strength and vitality, happiness, and inward peace. May the *real* Force be with you!

KNOCHEILISMS

PAUL'S LAW: You can't fall off the floor.

RUNE'S RULE: If you don't care where you are, you ain't lost.

BOOB'S LAW: You always find something the last place you look.

LAW OF THE SEARCH: The first place to look for anything is the last place you would expect to find it.

MARY-ANN'S LAW: You can always find what you're not looking for.

2—B.K.L.

CHAPTER 2
CODY'S CODICIL

People start pollution; people can stop it

Thousands of nautical miles from earth in the black void of space three astronauts in a gleaming, bell-shaped module raced against the clock. Traveling at incredible speed, Captain James A. Lovell, Jr., Jack Swigert, and Fred Haise, Jr. were trying to reach earth before their rapidly-dwindling supplies of oxygen, food, and water were gone.

The crisis began when a sudden explosion rocked the *Apollo 13*, cutting off most of the electrical power and other supplies aboard the moonbound spacecraft. A quick check by Lovell brought them face-to-face with the awful truth: There might not be sufficient life-support systems left for the trio to make it back to earth alive. The radio transmissions between Houston and the spacecraft were frantic. "What do we do now? Our power system is knocked out! How can we salvage the mission and save our lives?"

There were no quick or easy answers. But finally Houston informed them that there was a way the mission might be spared. Using the lunar module *Aquarius* as a life raft, the three astronauts, in conjunction with mission control, met the crisis with a series of improvisations that testify to human resourcefulness. With skill and nerve Lovell fired the engine of *Aquarius* to maneuver the spaceship into a "slingshot" course around the moon and back home to earth.

While mankind waited and prayed, Lovell, Swigert, and Haise concentrated on "consumables." The most immediately vital to them was oxygen. The three astronauts required about one pound of that life-giving element every three hours. After initial calculations Lovell discovered that there was sufficient oxygen for the return trip to earth. But another more serious problem soon became apparent. While there was enough oxygen to breathe in the environmental system of the small lunar module, *Aquarius* was inadequate to take care of what the men breathed out: carbon dioxide.

In our natural atmosphere carbon dioxide forms only about .03 percent—three parts in 10,000—of the total air. In normal operations aboard the spacecraft the CO_2 content is allowed to reach 33 times that amount, becoming 1 percent of the astronaut's atmosphere. But if the carbon dioxide level climbs to 2 percent, an astronaut's performance will begin to deteriorate after eight hours. If the spacemen continued to reuse air with ever higher amounts of CO_2 they would grow uncomfortable, then drowsy, and finally drop off to sleep—permanently.

The carbon dioxide is removed by filtering the air through canisters of lithium hydroxide, a compound that can absorb large amounts of carbon dioxide. *Aquarius* simply did not have enough lithium hydroxide to cleanse the waste air of three men for an extended length of time, but the command module *Odyssey* had two big cannisters. With careful instructions from mission control the astronauts rigged a pipeline from spacesuit hoses, friction tape, and cardboard to siphon the air through the lithium hydroxide in *Odyssey*. And so the air was scrubbed of the potentially lethal CO_2.

To add to their list of problems, water was in critically short supply. In fact, the astronauts consumed the last of their drinking water during their final day in space. A few more days and they might have suffered from dehydration, which causes deterioration from the resulting chemical imbalances in the body.

Because of the absolute necessity to conserve power, all equipment and systems outside *Aquarius* were turned off; and the temperature gradually dropped to below 50 degrees. Huddled in the cramped lunar module, the three voyagers tried to keep warm as they limped home in their stricken spaceship.

Some time later, after a succesful landing and recovery in the Pacific, Captain Lovell explained the ordeal to the members of the Senate Aeronautical and Space Sciences Committee. "It was a case of survival," he said quietly. "We were lucky. We survived."

So goes the story of the problem-plagued flight of *Apollo 13*—a mission which very nearly ended in disaster. And since that time men have wondered about the ultimate horror of being lost in space.

Martin Caidin, in his best-selling book *Marooned*, develops in his imagination what might happen if such an incident should ever occur. For with the exploration of the vertical frontier come unprecedented risks, not the least of which is the possibility of being marooned in the silent vastness of the universe without hope of rescue.

Could it ever happen? Could an astronaut be doomed to death by asphyxiation in a malfunctioning spacecraft? Could men be lost in space? A generation of Americans fascinated with space travel have asked these questions and wondered.

But let me tell you about another dilemma which we all face—a real and present danger which is not in the realm of fantasy or science fiction. For today we face a crisis almost identical to that faced by Lovell, Swigert, and Haise on the *Apollo 13* mission.

In a very real sense, we are all astronauts hurtling through space at incredible speed. Our space module is the earth. And, strange as it may seem, we discover that our life-support systems are running low. We are running out of clean air to breathe. We are running out of clean water to drink. Our food supply is perilously low. Our oil energy sources seem to be drying up. And without rescue we could perish, marooned in space, the victims of pollution, famine, and disease.

Ten years ago words like *pollution* and *environment* were on the fringe of our vocabulary, and very few of us knew the meaning of the word *ecology*. We know today that ecology is the study or science of the relationship of organisms to their habitat. We have been forced into this knowledge by the realization that our environment is rapidly deteriorating.

Today custodians of our natural resources are almost unanimous in warning us that unless our atmosphere, waters, and cities are redeemed and cleansed, life on this planet may not survive to the end of this century.

Millions of people join Professor Arthur Naftalin of the University of Minnesota and four-time mayor of Minneapolis, who is disillusioned with our "technocratic society." He claims that instead of feeding the world, we are retrogressing into the production of pollutants that are about to choke us to death.

Charles Reich, in his controversial book *The Greening of America*, highlights the complex problems of this generation. "People see it clearly," he asserts, "a society that . . . is ugly and artificial, which destroys the environment and the self. People shunted into insti-

22

tutional homes, streets made hideous with commercialism, the competitiveness and sterility of suburban living, the loneliness of the cities, the ruin to nature by bulldozers and pollution, the servile conformity, and the artificial quality of plastic lives in plastic homes.'' He goes on to say that America is being raped, robbed, and ripped off in a manner which litters our countrysides and renders our cities ugly and, in some parts, entirely uninhabitable.

And with each passing day the problems compound themselves as we continue to pollute and destroy the natural resources of our planet.

Cody's Codicil (named after Chief Iron Eyes Cody of the TV commercial) states, ''People start pollution, people can stop it.'' That is, mankind can solve the pollution dilemma through concerted human effort. It sounds good. And I am in complete agreement with the objectives of these ''save the environment'' programs. I long to see our trees, wildlife, air, water, etc., redeemed. Yet I seriously wonder if man possesses the capability of solving this critical enigma. For our whole society is interrelated with the problem of pollution.

What can we do about crudded-out rivers and steams, industrial waste, oil spills from offshore drilling, nuclear leakage from reactors and dump sites, tons of debris in our air, and excessive levels of carbon monoxide from automobiles? To change these things for the sake of the environment would mean altering the entire structure of our highly industrialized and technological society. And these changes will not come quickly; in fact, they may never occur at all.

Consider these statistics concerning the pollution of air and water—two essentials to the survival of man:

If air pollution continues at the present rate, in just

five years pollutants will have reduced the amount of sunlight reaching the earth by one half. No one has any idea what this will mean in terms of agriculture production, or what damage might be caused to all green, living things on earth.

It is estimated that 15 percent of everyone living in Los Angeles, California, now show noticeable, measurable pulmonary distress. Doctors cite air pollution as the major contributing factor.

Most of all our air pollution comes from transportation. But large amounts come also from power generation, industry, heating buildings, and trash burning. The total reaches 286 trillion pounds or 143 billion tons per year—in the air over our country alone. Our air is an unlicensed dump!

There is not enough oxygen for fish to survive in the Potomac River for twelve miles from Georgetown to Mt. Vernon. The bacteria count is 100 times the safe level to permit swimming.

An official, after seeing firsthand the clogged waste, oil residue, and debris in the Mississippi River, whimsically suggested that the river should be declared a fire hazard.

Water and air are just two resources which are succumbing to the effects of pollution. Multiply these problems a thousand times and you begin to grasp the enormity of our dilemma that affects the whole world.

One sad aspect of this ecological plight is the inability of many species to cohabit this planet with man. Several months ago my wife and I visited the Los Angeles Zoo in Griffith Park. I was amazed to note the variety of wildlife. But I was also alarmed to note many signs in front of the different cages—signs reading ENDANGERED SPECIES.

We have nearly wiped out the blue whale, the whooping crane, the African leopard. Passenger pigeons are now extinct, and the California condor is soon to join them. The great auk, the California grizzly bear, the great herds of American bison, the Carolina parakeet are all gone. We will never see these creatures again except in picture books.

Man is simply crowding these creatures off the planet. And naturalists who understand most deeply our relation to other living things know we cannot survive without our bird, fish, insect, and other animal life. But it is more than just a matter of diminishing numbers. As far as I am concerned it is also a matter of loneliness.

Can man go on indiscriminately destroying our natural resources and wildlife without ultimately doing irrepairable damage to himself?

Jacques Cousteau has spent his entire life in the study of the sea. He is a qualified marine biologist and naturalist who often speaks about the inherent dangers of pollution in terms of the world's oceans.

Recently I received a letter asking me to join the Cousteau Society—a group bent on reclaiming the seas and their resources. Now while I do not want to discuss the aims of this society, I do want to share with you some of Mr. Cousteau's observations. For in the letter he talks about what pollution of the oceans could ultimately mean in terms of man's survival.

He writes: "During the past thirty years I have observed and studied closely, and with my own two eyes I have seen the oceans sicken. Certain reefs that teemed with fish only ten years ago are almost lifeless. The ocean bottom has been raped by trawlers. Priceless wetlands have been destroyed by landfill. And everywhere are sticky globs of oil, plastic refuse, and unseen clouds of poisonous effluents. Often, when I describe the symptoms of the oceans' sickness, I hear remarks like 'they're only fish' or 'they're only whales' or 'they're only birds.' But I assure you that our destinies are linked with theirs in the most profound and fundamental manner. For if the oceans should die—by which I mean that all life in the sea would finally cease—this would signal the end not only for marine life, but for all other animals and plants of this earth as well, including man. With life departed, the oceans would become, in effect, one enormous cesspool. Billions of decaying bodies, large and small, would create such an insupportable stench that man would be forced to leave all the coastal regions. But far worse would follow. The ocean acts as the earth's buffer. It maintains a fine balance between the many salts and gases which make life possible. But dead seas would have no buffering effect. The carbon dioxide content of the atmosphere would start on a steady and remorseless climb; and when it reached a certain level, a 'greenhouse effect' would be created. The heat that normally radiates outward from the earth to space would be blocked by the CO_2, and sea-level temperatures would dramatically increase. One catastrophic effect of this heat would be melting of the ice caps at both the North and South Poles. As a result, the oceans would rise by a hundred feet or more, enough to flood almost all the world's major cities. These rising waters would drive one third of the earth's billions inland, creating famine, fighting, chaos, and disease on a scale almost impossible to imagine. Meanwhile, the surface of the ocean would have scummed over with a thick film of decayed matter, and would no longer be able to give water freely to the skies through evaporation. Rain would become a rarity, creating global drought and even more famine. But the final act is yet to come. The wretched remnant of the human race would now be packed cheek by jowl on the remaining highlands, bewildered, starving, struggling to survive hour by hour. Then would be visited upon them the final plague: anoxia [lack of oxygen]. This would be caused by the extinction of plankton algae and the reduction of land vegetation, the two sources that supply the oxygen you are now breathing. And so man would finally die, slowly gasping out his life on some barren hill. He would have survived the oceans by perhaps thirty years. And his heirs would be bacteria and a few scavenger insects."

So goes Jacques Cousteau's grim prediction on how the world might end. His description sounds like something from the book of Revelation telling about the final events which will convulse this planet just before the return of Christ.

But why do we have these pollution problems? Do you know that the Bible gives us the answer? I had always known that God's Word speaks on a variety of topics, but I never realized until recently that the Bible details for us why we have these ecological difficulties.

Listen to the words of the prophet Hosea, neither a scientist nor a naturalist. "Hear the word of the Lord. . . . The Lord has filed a lawsuit against you listing the following charges: There is no faithfulness, no kindness, no knowledge of God in your land. You swear and lie and kill and steal and commit adultery. There is violence everywhere, one murder after another. That is why your land is not producing; it is filled with sadness, and all living things grow sick and die; the animals, the birds, and even the fish begin to disappear." Hosea 4:1-4, LB.

Now these words were written to the nation of Israel centuries ago, but they find a striking application in the twentieth century. And notice, what reason does Scripture give for the desolation of the earth? The Bible states it is because of the sinfulness of man. Hosea said that the reason they had ecological problems was that they didn't know God. They were a wayward and perverse people.

You see, the Bible equates sin with the ecological problem. The Scripture parallels sin and pollution. And what we see in terms of the pollution of this planet is the result of the inner pollution of mankind.

All nature is confused. A curse seems to be upon all creation. And every year it makes itself more decidedly felt. The sin of man brought the sure result—decay, deformity, and death. Today the whole world is tainted, corrupted, stricken with moral disease. God's curse is upon the earth, upon man, upon the animals and the fish of the sea. And as the transgression becomes almost worldwide the curse will be permitted to become as broad and as deep as the transgression. The ecological problems we face are in direct ratio to our own sinfulness.

Now I am not a pessimist or a calamity howler, but I seriously doubt the truth of Cody's Codicil—"People start pollution, people can stop it." There is only one solution for pollution and that is Jesus Christ!

Twenty centuries ago, Jesus came to this polluted planet, lost in space, to redeem us from the harmful effects of sin. Though crucified on a cross, He rose again. And He promised to come back. And I believe His return is the only permanent solution for pollution.

You can think anything you want, but I believe man will never solve the pollution problem. He may try and even be partially successful, but he will never solve it completely. For you see, man can never solve the problem of sin. And until man can solve the sin problem he will be treating symptoms, not the disease—putting a band-aid on a cancer. Man can only change things, but God can change people.

The fact is, only Jesus Christ has the answer to the sin problem, the pollution problem, to every problem you face in life. And the only solution for pollution will come through Him who said, "Behold I create a new heavens and a new earth." Isaiah 65:17.

Centuries ago through the prophet, God spelled out the solution for pollution. It's a simple formula, yet effective. "If my people will humble themselves and pray, and search for me, and turn from their wicked ways, I will hear them from heaven and forgive their sins and heal their land." 2 Chronicles 7:14, LB.

METALAWS

THE CARDINAL CONUNDRUM: An optimist believes we live in the best of all possible worlds. A pessimist fears this is true.

BEDFELLOW'S RULE: The one who snores will fall asleep first.

SEIT'S LAW: The one course you must take to graduate will not be offered during your last semester.

KOVAC'S CONUNDRUM: When you dial a wrong number you never get a busy signal.

HAMILTON'S RULE FOR CLEANING GLASSWARE: The spot you are scrubbing is always on the other side.

DEVRIE'S DILEMMA: If you hit two keys on the typewriter, the one you don't want hits the paper.

GOLD'S LAW: If the shoe fits, it's ugly.

CHAPTER 3
KNOCHE'S CODICIL ON OBNOXIOUS PEOPLE

Those most in need of a good thrashing are invariably huge.

Rocko Marconi was a bad dude. He was worse than bad; he was the terror of the campus. Built like a Galion 24D earthmover, he possessed the fragile temperament of a wounded rhino. My roomate Jerry summed up Rocko's personality in a few words, "Marconi is like ten miles of bad road!"

To say that Rocko was obnoxious was a gross understatement. We called him by the nickname he preferred—"Rock." He called us whatever he wanted. If there was one thing bigger than Rocko's bulging biceps it was his oral cavity. He would constantly flaunt his clout by saying off-the-cuff, macho things like, "My mouth don't write no checks my body can't cash!" We would all laugh politely. This was preferable to becoming a makeshift hood ornament on his '65 Chevy Malibu.

Most of the time Rocko was tolerable, but occasionally he would exhibit various forms of socially unacceptable behavior. For instance, Rocko had this nasty habit of coming up behind you and planting his repugnant palm on your nape, saying, "Good to see you back!" (The word *back* being perfectly timed with the slap.) When this unpleasant experience occurred, one or both of two things was destined to happen: (1)

You would immediately lose consciousness; (2) You would bear a mammoth Rocko handprint for a fortnight. Ouch!

Generally Marconi and I got along. (Mainly because I avoided him like the plague.) But fate had dictated that there must be a showdown. It was to come all too soon.

It was the weekend of the lyceum. I had invited stunning Carmelita Malblotto to see Emil Norchild's classic film, "Paraguay—Jewel in the Navel of South America." It promised to be a grand and glorious evening.

During the course of the feature, I leaned over casually and whispered to Carmelita, "Hey, I never realized that Paraguay was the world's leading exporter of macrame furniture, did you?"

"Yes," she responded quietly.

"You actually knew that?" I queried.

"Sure. I saw this same lyceum program last year with Rocko."

"Rocko?" The name caught in my throat. "As in Rocko Marconi?"

"Yes, I thought you knew that Rocko and I were going together. The only reason I could go out with you tonight is that Rocko had a karate class. It's the Taekwondo exhibition. Rocko is demonstrating how to break concrete blocks with his bare hands. He'd kill you if he knew you had taken me out. But don't worry, Keith," she said sweetly. "I'll never tell."

I glanced over my shoulder and there, two rows back, was Lionel Snuglaster, Rocko's roommate. He grinned from ear to ear, knowingly, fiendishly.

"Oh, boy, I've really done it now," I thought, feeling a wave of terror. I broke into an involuntary tremble. My life flashed before me. I tried to erase the horrible vision from my brain—the picture of Rocko poised over me, my body a giant concrete block. I knew I was a man under sentence of death.

The rest of that evening was a blur of events. The movie could not end soon enough. I gave Carmelita an abbreviated Good-night and slunk back to the dorm. I knew that this slight indiscretion of dating Rocko's girl would ultimately mean pain—and I have a very low pain threshold.

Monday morning at 10:30 was my tennis class in the gym. I was in the locker room sitting on a bench tying my Pumas when I felt a huge hand on my shoulder. The hand squeezed, breaking several small bones in my neck. Realization. It was Rocko.

I smiled through my pain. "Nice day isn't it?"

"Yes," he agreed. "Almost twelve inches of rain since sunup."

"That's what I meant," I stammered. "It's a nice rain. It will help the . . . "

"Enough of this meteorological chit-chat," he interrupted. "Let's get down to business. My roommate Lionel tells me you were out with Carmelita last Saturday night. Is that true?"

I nodded, my chin quivering out of control.

"I wish you hadn't done that. Now I have to teach you a lesson," he said pulling me up two feet off the concrete by my collar.

The best defense is a good offense, someone has said, so I decided to try to intimidate him by a show of brute strength. Springing loose, I poised ready to strike. Holding my hands in karate fashion, I said, "Rocko, I am required by law to warn you that my hands are lethal weapons registered with the U.S. government and that should you try to start anything I would be . . ."

Before I could finish my sentence the fight began. Thrusting my nose firmly between his teeth, I threw him to the ground heavily on top of me. I pummelled his knee with my stomach and climaxed the bout by giving him a crushing blow on his fist with my chin. Lights out. That's all I remember before losing consciousness.

When I awoke, Rocko was gone; the locker room empty. My body was a mass of bruised and aching flesh. I hobbled back to the dorm to nurse my wounds.

That was my first and last encounter with Rocko, mainly because it was my first and last date with Carmelita. I understand that Rocko and Carmelita were married last June. They deserved each other. All's swell that ends swell.

Since that experience years ago I have met many obnoxious people, but, to date, Rocko Marconi still is at the top of the heap. Knoche's Codicil on obnoxious people states: "Those most in need of a good thrashing are invariably huge." In truth, this has been born out in real life.

But what do you do? How do you handle tough characters and tough situations like that? I often wonder how Jesus would have dealt with Rocko Marconi. But then I think I know, because the Bible spells it out for us.

In Matthew 5:39, 44 (TEV), we read about Christ's attitude. "If anyone slaps you on the right cheek, let him slap your left cheek too." "Love your enemies."

Jesus here is contrasting the Old Testament principle of "eye for eye, tooth for tooth" (Exodus 21:23-25), the law of retaliation, with a new principle which dictates that His followers be guided by a spirit of love. "A new commandment I give you," He said, "that you love one another." John 13:34, RSV.

33

For centuries people have ridiculed the advice of Jesus, "Love your enemies" (Matthew 5:44), as being impractical, idealistic, and absurd. Yet today, psychiatrists, physicians, and religionists are recommending it as a panacea for many of man's ills. When Jesus said, "Forgive seventy times seven" (see Matthew 18:22), He was enunciating sound spiritual principles that contribute to a healthy body and mind.

The person who is controlled by the spirit of self-centeredness, resentment, hatred, and revenge is not happy. In fact, such an attitude can actually adversely affect one's physical health and well-being.

King Solomon must have known about this when he declared, "Better a dish of vegetables, with love, than the best beef served with hatred." Proverbs 15:17, Moffatt.

Do you remember when James and John, the Sons of Thunder, wanted Jesus to call down fire on a Samaritan village because the people refused to give them lodging? These disciples were believers in and followers of Jesus. Yet, these Christians, smarting from the sting of racial discrimination, were so full of hatred and revenge that they asked the Lord to do a repeat of the Sodom and Gomorrah bit. But Jesus rebuked them by saying, "Ye know not what manner of spirit ye are of." Luke 9:55.

Before Pentecost, Peter also was possessed by the fiery spirit of vengeance. In the Garden of Gethsemane, convulsed by anger and hatred, he tried to cut off the head of one of the soldiers. But wound up clipping off an ear. When provoked, Peter's first reaction was to hurt. And when he did, Jesus reached out and touched the ear and made it whole. Jesus' first instinct was to heal.

What a transformation occurred in James, John, and

Peter after they crucified self and were filled with the Holy Spirit. The old spirit of getting even was replaced by the Holy Spirit of Christ who, when He was reviled, reviled not again.

Do we have that kind of attitude, that kind of spirit? Or have we, in our conversations, been trying to cut off heads or call down fire upon those who have given us a rough time? How do you and I react when someone either purposely or ignorantly does something we don't like? An honest appraisal should make it clear whether we possess the Holy Spirit in our lives.

Booker T. Washington went down to Alabama to found the Tuskegee Institute. He came across bitter racial prejudice against his blackness. One day he was walking down a road past a beautiful southern mansion, when a woman came out on the porch and hollered at him, "Hey, boy! Boy! I need some firewood cut!"

Without a word, Booker T. Washington walked to the woodpile, took off his coat, chopped an armload of wood, and even carried it into the house.

When he was gone, one of the servants got up enough courage to go to the woman of the house and say, "Madam, that was Booker T. Washington!" And to the woman's credit she was genuinely ashamed. She headed for the Tuskegee Institute to find the professor. When she apologized, Washington smiled and said, "Madam, there's no apology needed. I enjoy doing favors for my friends."

Here was a man who refused to let others' attitudes toward him influence his attitude toward them. Have you become that Christlike? Or do you simply like people because they like you? To be like Jesus is not to allow our attitude toward others to be merely a reflection of their attitudes toward us.

You may have bitter resentments in your heart. Maybe there's even a Rocko Marconi in your past haunting you. Won't you let Jesus take that self-centeredness and rancor and hatred away? Let the Holy Spirit perform the divine surgery to remove the disease-producing spirit of retaliation.

"So put to death those members that are on earth." "Once you moved among them, when you lived in them; but off with them all now, off with anger, rage, malice, slander! . . You have stripped off the old nature with its practices, and put on the new nature." "Be clothed with compassion, kindliness, humility, gentleness, and good temper—forbear and forgive each other in any case of complaint; as Christ forgave you, so must you forgive. And above all you must be loving, for love is the link of the perfect life." Colossians 3:5, 7-10, 12-14, Moffatt.

CHAPTER 4
ROOSEVELT'S
REVELATION

We have nothing to fear but fear itself.

Recently, while browsing one afternoon in Norfziger's bookstore down on Second Street, I spied a volume I simply had to have. Its red-lettered cover literally leaped out at me. It was entitled: "How to Understand Yourself," by Dr. Ceril S. Jongwad, noted psychiatrist, psychologist, pioneer in Gestalt Therapy and Transactional Analysis, and distributor of beanbag furniture. The subtitle of the book intrigued me—"Uncover the Most Intimate Truths About Yourself." Since I have never really known myself (although I have become pretty well acquainted with my legs), I plopped down the $2.95 for the paperback.

At home I scanned the preface. The book turned out to be a collection of psychological tests, quizzes, and games that you take and score yourself. In the table of contents, the chapter headings drew me deeper into the complex world of my own psyche—"Analyzing Your Dreams," "How Creative Are You?" "Developing Your Memory," "How Brave Are You?" Aha! That was where I'd begin. After all, I reasoned, I am a brave and courageous soul. Surely I would soar above my fellows on the Bravery Scale.

I turned to page 96, and began to read: "Everyone experiences fear to some degree or another. Any per-

son incapable of this emotion would not survive long in what is essentially a hostile and dangerous world. However, there are marked differences in the way people respond to fear. These responses can be broken down into two major categories—'rational' and 'irrational' fears. The following test, if you answer the questions objectively, will reveal how fearful a person you are—whether your fears are 'real' or 'imagined.' Now, answer each question and score your answers on a separate sheet of paper. Ready? Begin.''

Multiple-Choice Section

1. You are in your doctor's office for a routine checkup. As your physician listens intently with his stethoscope to your heart, you hear him say, ''uh oh!'' Is your first reaction to:

a. Shrug it off, knowing that the doctor was merely clearing his throat.

b. Begin drafting your ''Last Will and Testament.''

c. Scream at the top of your lungs, ''I don't want to die!''

2. A friend, whom you know to be a top-notch pilot and keen on aerobatics, offers you a ride in his own light plane. In a dangerous powerdive at 350 m.p.h. and six G's, he loses control. As the plane plummets earthward, your last thought would be:

a. Shucks, and I just bought two tickets to the ice show.

b. Those people look like ants down there—sure, big ants—about the size of sheep—er, I mean cattle—

c. Help! Where's my parachute!

3. You have been given an opportunity to ride in a midget submarine with famed undersea explorer Jacque La Jacque. At a depth of 22,000 feet off the coast of Japan, a hairline crack develops in the sub's

superstructure. Water begins to seep, then suddenly pour in. With death imminent, you say:

a. "It's okay, I needed a bath."

b. "Jacque, is your middle name really La?"

c. "Let me out of this deathtrap. I can't die without fulfilling my lifelong dream—to never die!"

4. Your car has broken down in the country near a large, private house. You casually stroll up the driveway to ask for help. Suddenly, a huge Great Dane appears with his teeth bared, running straight for you. Just as he is about to bury his fangs in your calf, you respond this way:

a. You say, "Nice doggy. Want to play chase the fountain pen?"

b. You stand motionless as a statue hoping the canine won't notice you.

c. You break the current world record for the 100-yard dash as you run screaming back to your car.

5. For a bet, you have agreed to spend the night on your own in a wax museum. Your bed has been set up in the dimly lit "Chamber of Horrors." As you lie down to go sleepy-bye, your thoughts would be:

a. I wonder what blood type Dracula prefers? (Hopefully not type A—yours!)

b. What is that horrific pounding noise? (You suddenly realize it is your own heart beating wildly in your chest.)

c. Help! I want my mummy!

Yes-or-No Section

1. Would you like to participate in a "dangerous sport" such as skydiving, shark hunting, or squirrel rustling?

2. Do you find the idea of standing in the center of a bullfighting arena in a Santa suit unsettling?

3. Does the thought of washing outside windows on the 103rd floor of the Empire State Building cause you to drop your squeegee?

4. Would you take a ride in an untethered balloon, if you knew that during the flight, you'd be forced to eat pasteurized cheese?

5. Do you feel nervous or fearful at the thought of taking this test?

After completing the test, I checked the score grid in the back of the book to see how I made out. To my amazement, I didn't score very high on the Bravery Scale. In fact, on the score grid, zero being ''coward'' and ten being ''dare-devil,'' I peaked out at about 2.5. (Not a total pansy, but then not the Incredible Hulk either.)

The test results are in, and the truth is out. I'm not all that brave after all. I guess I have to be content to suffer along with my fellow human beings, feeling the insecurity, frustration, and fear that comes with membership in a *Homo sapiens*. For all of us experience this emotion throughout a lifetime.

Fear can take many forms. Fear of failure. Fear of growing old. Fear of loss of love. Fear of death. We all are afraid of someone or something, the shapeless shadows that lurk in the darkness. No one is immune from this emotion.

But it is comforting to know that there is a God in heaven who understands our fears. And what's more, He removes our fears.

In the twenty-third psalm, the shepherd's psalm, we read these words, ''The Lord is my shepherd; I shall not want. He maketh me to lie down in green pastures: he leadeth me beside the still waters.''

In Palestine there are many streams and rivulets in

the high country where David herded his sheep. But the water is rushing down toward the valley. And sheep are afraid to approach rushing water.

There is good reason for this. The wool on a sheep's back is mighty handy in the cold, and it even serves nicely as insulation against the heat. But it isn't fit for water. And should the sheep's wool overcoat get wet, the sheep could easily drown. The sheep knows instinctively that it must fear rushing water.

But the shepherd understands the sheep's fear, and that is why he leads his flock beside the still waters. And if there isn't a quiet pool nearby, then he gets to work with some rocks and sticks and mud and builds a small dam. Then he leads his sheep beside the still waters.

The Good Shepherd first understands your fear, and then He removes all need for fear.

Maybe you are fearful that you won't have enough money to pay the bills. Jesus says, Don't be afraid. "Seek ye first the kingdom of God, . . . and all these things shall be added unto you." Matthew 6:33.

It is possible that you're afraid of world conditions and the imminent threat of nuclear war. Jesus says, Don't be afraid. "Behold, I come quickly." Revelation 22:7.

Some of us are afraid of sickness. Jesus says in effect, "Don't be afraid. I am the Great Physician."

Perhaps you are afraid of growing old. Jesus says, Don't be afraid. "Behold, I make all things new." Revelation 21:5.

Roosevelt's Revelation states: "We have nothing to fear but fear itself." But when we are secure in God's love we have nothing to fear at all. "There is no fear in love; but perfect love casteth out fear." 1 John 4:18.

Our heavenly Father first understands our fear. And

then, in His love, He removes all fear. I'm glad we have a God like that, aren't you?

APPLIED METALAWS

ANDERSON'S THEOREM: If at first you don't succeed, you are running about average.

DONNA'S LAW OF PURCHASE: If you want it, and you can't afford it, buy it—it won't be there when you go back.

CORRY'S LAW: Paper is always strongest at the perforations.

OZARD'S RAIN RULE: The amount of rain is directly proportional to the length of time your raincoat is at the dry cleaners.

CHAPTER 5
NOODLEMAN'S
OBSERVATION

Tact is the knack of pulling the stinger from the bee
without getting stung.

Tactfulness is an art. It is a form of diplomacy every
man and woman must master who would be truly successful. The wise man Solomon put it this way, "A
man of tact is popular." Proverbs 13:15, Moffatt. Or as
the Revised Standard Version puts it, "Good sense
wins favor."

Noodleman observed that "tact is the knack of pulling the stinger from the bee without getting stung."
There is a lot of truth in that adage; and some years ago
my father proved that lesson to me in a remarkable
way.

We were living in a nice California community; and
the members of Dad's church rendered due hospitality
to the pastor and his family Sabbath by Sabbath. One
particular Saturday morning, we arrived at church
early, parked the car, and were greeted by none other
than Corbett Snavely. Now Corbett had a reputation
as a self-styled gourmet cook. He owned a local health-
food store and was constantly experimenting with new
combinations of nutritious foods. To say that he was a
health nut would be a gross understatement. To put it
simply, he was a health fanatic.

In the parking lot that morning, Corbett presented
Dad with a huge pot containing his latest dietary deli-

cacy—herb stew. Dad thanked Mr. Snavely for his kind gift and proceeded to place the pot in the trunk of the car. We would take it home and have it for our noon meal that day.

Little did we know what lurked within the confines of that covered caldron. None of us had tasted herb stew before; but we would give it a try. This seemed to please Corbett, as his countenance radiated a warm glow of satisfaction.

After the service we got in the car to go home for lunch. The whole car interior was permeated with a strange stench. Dad suspected the herb stew. He was right. We opened the windows and drove home.

At home Dad opened the trunk and removed the pot of potent porridge. He took it into the kitchen and set the container on the counter. We all stood around as he lifted the lid. Noxious fumes filled the house. My mother's prize Boston fern a full ten feet away gasped, wilted, and died.

Finally, when most of the odor had disseminated, we all ventured closer to peer down into the putrid kettle. What greeted my eyes can hardly be expressed with pen and paper, but I shall try. The base substance of the stew was a gelatinous ooze that closely resembled mud. In this gluggy brown mass swam assorted plant life. The whole was garnished with watercress, grass shoots, seaweed, and what looked like fossilized earthworms. Blee-ah!

We all stood there for a moment—speechless. Then Dad suggested that perhaps one of us should sample this concoction. Who would be the guinea pig? Mom volunteered. She took only a smidgen of the foreign matter on a spoon and placed it in her mouth. Her smiling visage was instantly changed. (Shades of Dr. Jekyl and Mr. Hyde.) Her facial muscles contorted. She grabbed her throat. "That stuff is awful!" she coughed.

We were all satisfied with her appraisal.

"Well, what are we going to do with it?" I asked. As if in answer to our prayer, into the kitchen walked our beagle, Claude.

"Let's let Claude eat it. He'll eat anything," my sister suggested. And it was true, Claude could devour just about anything. He was more like a billy goat than a canine. Surely he would demolish this nurture as he would any other festive board.

Mom spooned a healthy (?) portion into Claude's dish. We set the dish down on the floor under his nose. He took one quick, discriminating sniff, turned up his nose, and walked away in cool contempt. Bad news!

Now what were we going to do?

A thought flashed into my fertile cranium. "Why not use it like mulch around some of the plants in the front yard?" I didn't hit pay dirt. Mom remembered the Boston fern.

"Well," Dad said in exasperation, "we have got to get rid of it."

He had no other option but to pour the raunchy regimen down the garbage disposal. With very little ceremony, he flipped on the switch and proceeded to dump the chow down the gurgling pit. There was one anxious moment when even the disposal seemed to falter, as if not to accept our offering. It coughed, sputtered, and the herb stew was gone.

That eliminated the problem for the present. But doubts loomed. How would Dad answer when Corbett asked how we enjoyed his special herb stew? I waited with bated breath to see what would happen next Sabbath morning.

All too soon Sabbath arrived. Sure enough, when we

got to church Corbett Snavely was waiting to ask the inevitable question.

As Dad was walking in the front door of the church, Corbett confronted him, "Well, pastor, what did you think? How did you like the herb stew?"

There was a moment of silence as Dad gathered his words. A minister must not lie. He must speak truth. I held my breath.

Finally he answered. "Corbett," he said. "That was truly a unique dish. Frankly, I've never tasted anything like it. You should have seen it go down!"

I breathed again, and Mr. Snavely beamed with delight. "Talk about diplomat Henry Kissinger, why Dad made him look like a rank amateur," I thought to myself. And to this day I have always admired the tactfulness with which my father handled that situation.

Now please don't misunderstand. We should never tell a lie. The point is that people and their feelings are important. So often in our relations with one another we do not exercise tactfulness. In an effort to be candid or frank we may injure someone's tender feelings and render it virtually impossible to be of Christian witness to them. How much better to be tactful.

The strongest argument in favor of the gospel is a loving and lovable Christian. In the process of being tactful, you will be both loving and lovable.

Dad could have been frank with that member and told him flat out that he didn't like his stew—that we couldn't stomach it. But he didn't. Why? Because he loved Corbett as a brother and friend. And because he didn't want to unduly hurt his feelings, he was tactful.

"Be kindly affectionate one to another with brotherly love; in honour preferring one another." Romans 12:10. "Beloved, if God so loved us, we ought also to love one another." 1 John 4:11.

CHAPTER 6
LAW OF
PROCRASTINATION

Procrastination avoids boredom; one never has the feeling that there is nothing important to do.

Wanita Fullenwider was a rare breed. She was the only girl on campus whose major was musicology and whose minor was auto mechanics. In addition, she boasted a brown belt in karate, could speak fluent Swahili, and once played viola in the Snoot String Quartet. Was I impressed!

I'll never forget the first time I saw her. She was sucking on a straw, siphoning gas out of a lawn mower. She worked on the campus grounds crew. She was stunning with her fiery green eyes, blond hair, and well-tanned, leatherlike skin. She asked me if I wanted to see a few karate moves. I nodded. Then with a terrifying scream—"H-e-e-a-a-ah!"—she lashed out at me with flailing hands and feet. I laughed lightly at the resultant abrasions. What a girl!

"Hey, Keith," she said catching her breath. "Why don't you and I go on the hayride together this Saturday night. It would be a panic!"

"Well, you see, Wanita," I groped for words. "I have this biology paper due. I have to write a report on the armadillo for Dr. Bland's class."

"Dr. Maxine Bland?" she retorted. "Why, she's the worst teacher in the whole bio department. I think she's gross!" Wanita stuck out her pink tongue.

"That may be," I responded. "But like it or not, I have to have that 500-word theme in by a week from Monday. And I had better get cracking."

"Keith, you dumb oaf," she laughed. "Don't you know anything?" Then she produced a small card and handed it to me.

"What's that?" I asked.

"What's that! It's a special library pass card. My roommate, Valma Fronaberger, works in the library and got it for me. This card means that I have access to the stacks."

"Stacks?"

"Yeah, the stacks! I—I mean *we* can go into the room where they keep all the themes, reports, term papers. Don't you see? There is bound to be some kind of a report or paper on the armadillo. You'll have all the information you need. You can get it done in a fraction of the time. That, of course, will allow us enough time to go to the hayride. OK?"

"I—I—I don't know," I said with an air of caution.

"Look," she said taking my hand in hers, "would you rather know a bunch of dumb facts about the armadillo? Or would you rather get to know me?"

It hit me with sinus-clearing clarity. "I'd rather get to know you," I managed.

"Good. Then pick me up Saturday night at seven o'clock. Don't be late."

I felt a bit nervous about my decision. I knew I needed to finish the report. But then I had over a week. Surely things would work out.

The Saturday-night hayride was blissful with Wanita by my side. But that was only the beginning. The following week we were out every night—a trip to the shopping mall, an evening in the student center TV room, a karate tournament. That week was a blur.

50

Occasionally fear would dart through my mind like a lizard across a hot rock. Then I would say to myself, "Keith, you still have several more days to do that report. Relax and enjoy yourself. You deserve it."

The week dwindled. All too soon it was Friday. I awoke, as it were, in Dr. Bland's biology class.

Maxine Bland was one of those college professors who had been teaching for thirty years. Her silver gray hair was mute testimony to the rigors of the teaching trade. She knew her craft, and she would not tolerate student laziness. "Now, don't forget," she prompted. "There is a 500-word report due first thing Monday morning. You each have been assigned topics. No excuses will be accepted for late themes. Class dismissed."

As I ambled from the classroom, who should I run into but Wanita.

"Hiya, Keith," she gleamed. "You're just the person I wanted to talk to."

"Oh, yeah," I mumbled.

"Yeah," she continued. "Keith, you simply won't believe it! The greatest thing is happening this Saturday night! The Museum of Modern Art is having a special exhibition. It's a showing of the works of sculptor Odilon Redon."

"Who's he?" I queried, exposing a cultural Achilles' heel that runs up my leg to the back of my neck.

"You're kidding, aren't you?" She chuckled and waved a pamphlet. "It says right here that Odilon Redon is the greatest living exponent of metal sculpture. He is the master who is famous for his *Impacted Buick*—one of the finest examples of the modern emphasis on the precise interplay of chrome nuance and pastel shading. He is, in a word, fabulous! Keith, can't we take in this exhibition? It's one night only."

"Wanita, have you forgotten? I have a theme due Monday morning. This is not the kind of thing I can chisel out in a couple of hours. I've got to get started!"

"How long does it have to be?"

"Five hundred words."

"Then no hassle. We'll begin on Sunday. It's a cinch."

"Wanita, I don't know if I can crank it out in one day. Don't forget, I'm not very bright."

"Yes, I know," she agreed. "But even you should be able to write a simple 500-word theme in a day. Come on, now. Quit worrying about it and pick me up Saturday night at seven. Bye."

I gritted my teeth. "I'm going to regret this," I said to myself.

The Modern Art Exhibit of Odilon Redon was wonderfully weird. The highlight was his *Impacted Buick*— demonstrating the delicate ambiguity of a crunched car. Wanita floated in seventh heaven. I survived.

Sunday dawned bright and clear. My alarm clock didn't go off, so I climbed out of the sack late. One thing and another demanded my time until, at dusk, I was themeless.

"Keith . . . Pssst . . . Keith," I opened my dorm window. Outside on the front lawn was Wanita. "Come on. We've got to get to the library. It closes in two hours. Hurry and we'll get you a theme paper from the stacks. Get a move on!"

I grabbed my binder and a couple of pens and headed for the lobby. Wanita met me and we were off to the library.

As we jogged along she spoke, "Keith, some grad students and seniors get stack permits. They're able to go through old themes, papers, and reports when they're doing the kind of work that requires a great deal of research. Normally students don't have access to this material, but Valma got us two passes. We'll go in, present the passes, and once in the stacks we'll find a paper on the armadillo. Then, I'll be lookout while you copy the report. It's foolproof!''

"You can't be serious!" I countered. "If Dr. Bland ever finds out they'll lock me up for life!"

"Keith," Wanita said in a serious tone, "you've messed around now all week and haven't gotten it done. Now you have no choice."

"Oh, brother, how did I get into this?" I thought to myself.

Just as Wanita had said, the permits got us into the inner recesses of the library. The stacks filled me with awe. Thousands of themes, reports, and theses were filed on metal shelves. The shelves were several tiers high and stretch to the ceiling. Ladders on wheels were used to reach the highest shelves.

"Come on. Hurry," said Wanita. "The biology section is in the back, the first tier. Here it is. Now, look for a theme that has a lot of dust on it."

I fumbled through the folders until I found a biology paper in a faded green binder. Title: "The Habits and Habitat of Mr. Armadillo" by Zola Abercrombie. "Hey, Wanita," I whispered excitedly, "this just might do the trick!"

Wanita opened the binder cover and looked at the record card in the envelope pasted inside the cover. "This is no good," she said. "The card shows that this paper was checked out last year. There's always a chance Dr. Bland has seen it. We want a paper that hasn't been checked out for at least ten years; then we'll be safe."

"Right," I agreed.

After looking for several more minutes, Wanita

made a real find. It was a theme paper of ideal length that hadn't been checked out since October 22, 1946. Title: "The Armadillo—Nature's Tank" by M. Efird.

"This is perfect!" Wanita said ecstatically. "And since it hasn't been checked out since 1946, the chance of Dr. Bland's having seen it are commensurate with finding two identical snowflakes. No hassle with plagiarism."

"Plagiarism!" I shot back. "You didn't say anything about plagiarism! Wanita, this whole thing has gone far enough! I want out! I mean it!" But as I raged impotently the back of my thigh tightened, and I was forced to sit.

"Keith, you supercilious twit. Get ahold of yourself," Wanita scolded. "No one is ever going to find out. Here's pen and paper. Now start copying. And hurry. The library closes in less than an hour."

Great drops of sweat beaded on my forehead. My hand trembled as I began to write. It started like this:

"Since primordial times, homo sapiens have pondered a diminutive quadruped with a coat of mail, a distant link to hoary dinosaurs that languished in dank lagoons and swarthy troughs, a nocturnal mammal of amazing agility and alacrity, who, when maliciously assailed by a host of blood-thirsty predators, has harped back to an indigenous cunning from aforetimes, and rolling into a ball, has repelled the mad foray of wroth carnivores and even man, who sought his savory flesh for their beneficent gruels."

"I can't turn in this stuff!" I said to Wanita. "It just doesn't sound like me!"

"Don't be finicky. Write!" Wanita commanded.

I scribbled down the words furiously until the entire report was complete. Thirty seconds before it closed, we exited from the library.

Once outside, I took Wanita to task. "I should have never listened to you! I could get arrested for plagiarism. Or worse, kicked out of school! I just have bad vibes about this whole thing!"

"You're a worrywart," Wanita consoled. "Relax. Everything will work out just fine. You'll see."

Monday morning in biology class I submitted my report—a word-for-word rendering of M. Efird's "The Armadillo—Nature's Tank." I felt sick to my stomach. I couldn't concentrate on the day's lecture. I felt like I was in a time warp. When class was over I headed back to the dorm and fell into bed.

All week long I was worried and depressed. I realized that my own procrastination had caused this whole ugly mess. I hated myself. In fact, I had even progressed into advanced stages of self-loathing. I felt lower than a gopher's basement.

Friday. Fear turned to dread. We were to get the results of our biology reports. I was prepared for the worst. I wasn't even surprised when Dr. Bland asked me to stay after class.

"I want to talk to you about your theme, Mr. Knoche," said Professor Bland when we were alone in the room. "Most interesting!"

"Oh?" I gulped.

"Yes,' she continued, "you have a most unusual writing style. It's really quite unique—an archaic flavoring, a lean objectivity, a sensitivity and perception unlike any student I've had in my tenure in this institution of learning."

"Just lucky I guess," I said with an air of humility.

"Oh, you're much too modest about your gift, Mr. Knoche. I haven't seen such prosaic penmanship since . . . say . . . 1946. I believe the student's name was Maxine Efird."

"Maxine Efird?" I said, my voice hitting high C.

"Yes, Maxine was a freshman biology major then. She even went on to get her doctorate. Of course, Efird was her maiden name until she married her college sweetheart, Macalester Bland."

Suddenly it all came together, like the vortex of a great whirlpool, or giant planets colliding—KABOOM! I experienced what Jean-Paul Satre so fondly referred to as "nothingness." I was struck with a profound sense of despair and was vividly reminded of the diaries sometimes left by doomed explorers lost at the south pole, or letters from German soldiers at Stalingrad. I was dead.

"Don't look so crestfallen, Mr. Knoche," Professor Bland said, momentarily rousing me from the slough of self-pity. "Believe it or not, I was rather flattered that someone considered my paper worthy to be used as, shall we say, source material. I had almost forgotten about 'The Armadillo—Nature's Tank.' It's been so many years! It's hard to believe I could have written that badly." She glanced at my theme and read, "The mad foray of wroth carnivores and even man, who sought his savory flesh for their beneficent gruels." She smiled and said, "Simply awful, isn't it?"

I nodded agreement, then disagreement, looking like a ceramic figurine that sits in the rear car window, its head bobbing about on a spring. As I continued to bob, Dr. Bland again spoke.

"Mind you, I don't think what you did was right, Mr. Knoche! Plagiarism is a serious offense. Far better to use several sources when preparing your next research paper. I trust you won't make the same mistake again. I will have to dock you a grade point. But I will allow you one additional week to prepare an original theme on the subject. Fair enough?"

I nodded and bobbed vigorously, this time in the affirmative. Scurrying from the classroom, I made my way directly to the library. I was going to begin that afternoon to draft my original theme on the armadillo. No more procrastination!

That one experience helped me revolutionize my study habits. I began to budget my time and regulate my daily schedule. And I was amazed at the results. My G.P.A. soared like a kite on a crisp March wind.

The Law of Procrastination suggests: "Procrastination avoids boredom; one never has the feeling that there is nothing important to do." That's true, even when you're up at 2 a.m. on No-Doz, trying to crank out a research paper you neglected to do. Procrastination is a downer. Take it from me!

Look. It just makes sense to plan ahead, to get your priorities straight, to put first things first. Procrastination is deadly when you're trying to get an education. And it's even more fatal in the spiritual life.

The world is brimful of procrastinators with good intentions. They know that they need to take time for God—but they're too busy. They know they need to develop real Christian character to withstand life's trials, and they're going to do it—but they don't have time right now. They realize that Jesus is coming soon and they need to prepare to meet Him—but not today. And urgent things, by their very nature, crowd out the important. The kingdom of God becomes a "low-priority" item.

This "mañana" philosophy, often called the "I'll-do-it-tomorrow" syndrome, has grave implications in terms of a person's eternal destiny.

I think that Jesus was addressing Himself to this very issue when He told the parable of the ten bridesmaids. Five of the bridesmaids were wise and filled their lamps with oil, while the other five were foolish and forgot. So when the bridegroom arrived, after some delay, the foolish bridesmaids faced a serious oil shortage. They had to leave the wedding party to buy fuel for their lamps. On the other hand, the wise bridesmaids were prepared and went into the marriage feast. "Later, when the other five returned, they stood outside, calling, 'Sir, open the door for us!'

"But he called back, 'Go away! It is too late!'"

"So stay awake and be prepared, for you do not know the date or moment of my return." Matthew 25:11-13, LB.

The point of Jesus' story cannot be ignored. The second coming is near. Christ, the bridegroom, is about to return. Those who procrastinate, who are unprepared at the time of His arrival, will not only be disappointed, they will be lost.

Don't you think it's time to make a new priority list, making God number one? Don't hesitate! Don't procrastinate! "Seek ye first the kingdom of God." Matthew 6:33. Don't wait! Do it now!

KNOCHEOLOGY

SINTETO'S FIRST LAW: A sixty-day warranty guarantees that the product will self-destruct on the sixty-first day.

BALANCE'S LAW: How long a minute is depends on which side of the bathroom door you're on.

MOSER'S LAW: Exciting plays occur only while you are watching the scoreboard or out buying popcorn.

LAW OF LIFE'S HIGHWAY: If everything is coming your way, you're in the wrong lane.

CHAPTER 7
McMILLAN'S
INVERSE LAW OF
CONSUMABLES:

It's not what you eat—it's what eats you.

Minor annoyances usually can be shrugged off. But a host of indignities to the mind and to the spirit that you face in the course of a normal day can make you want to literally tear your hair out by the roots. Consider the following "stressful situations" that could make you just scream:

● Finding out someone you always thought was useless and inept is making three times your salary.

● Going to the doctor and realizing your home scale is five pounds light.

● Standing in the supermarket express line behind someone who brazenly totes more than nine items.

● Accidently snapping off your TV antenna.

● People who greet your great news with begrudging remarks like, "Oh really," and then change the subject.

● Typing a flawless letter, and then ending with "Simcerely."

● Playing golf or tennis with a person who can't resist giving unsolicited instructions on how to improve your game.

● Bringing home a new plant and watching it die an agonizing death the following week.

● Getting a telephone call from someone who, as

soon as you answer, says, "Please hold."

● Being told to "Go with the flow" in the midst of a personal crisis.

● Getting off the plane first and being rewarded by getting your luggage back last.

● Making a doctor's appointment for 9 a.m. and sitting in the waiting room until 10:30.

● Trying to get help from a salesperson who answers every question with, "I don't know," "I don't work in this department," or "All we have is just what's out."

● Receiving a "Final Warning" notice on a bill when there was never a first warning.

Such "stressful situations" are the stuff of life. Most of us when faced with the prospect of encountering these difficulties, have determined to muddle through. It's part of that thing called the Puritan Ethic we're supposed to have inherited. Work and you will succeed. Dream the impossible dream. Every frog is an unkissed prince.

Dare to be great, they tell us. And so we stroll down life's highway, eyes to the sky, oblivious to the chuckholes underfoot—and, believe me, there are chuckholes! Mother Nature is remarkably evenhanded in dishing up the lumps with the gravy.

But how do you handle the hassles, the tensions, the stresses and strains of everyday life?

Well, first off we must learn that not all stress is bad. Some is even beneficial. No one can escape it, for without stress life would be impossible. A baby is born under stress. A child sitting up for the first time is under stress. So is an athlete trying to win a race, an artist performing on stage, a student facing a final examination.

What is important is not so much the stress itself but how we react to it.

Recently a Stress Test was given in Cleveland, Ohio. Portable electrocardiographs were attached to various professionals to measure the impact of stress on the heart. The researchers measured cardiac stress in surgeons performing life-and-death operations, in lawyers in the heat of courtroom trials, in television broadcasters meeting deadline schedules, in high-powered advertising men, and in skydivers. The results were fascinating. It was shown that it was not the high-tension job that produced emotional stress, but the individual's attitude. A nervous, high-strung person can develop heart stress even in a seemingly placid job in a library, while an imperturbable tycoon with three telephones ringing at once can take stress in stride.

What made the difference? Attitude. What makes stress helpful or hurtful? How we react to life's stress situations. We hold the key and can decide whether stress is going to work for us or against us, make us "better or bitter."

On one hand, when stress becomes greater than the body can tolerate it can cause serious psychosomatic responses: heart trouble, stomach problems leading to ulcers, respiratory ailments, headaches, and so on. On the other hand, properly handled, stress can promote mental stability and physical health and can better equip us to deal with the next set of pressures that comes along. But in a very real sense, we decide the outcome. Hence, McMillans' Inverse Law of Consumables: "It's not what you eat—it's what eats you." While proper diet is necessary, a healthy emotional attitude is vital.

Given the stern dicta of reality, how can *Homo sapiens*, that frail clod with an overbite and no pelt, ever manage to maintain a healthy emotional attitude in this hostile environment? Here is where Christianity comes galloping to the rescue. The religion of Jesus provides mankind with a secret weapon, more powerful than Mother Nature's most malevolent molecule. The secret weapon is faith. It's a type of complete trust in God that causes us to laugh at life's troubles, retain our sanity, and keep trudging after the grail.

This firm reliance in God is fact, not fantasy. It is a dynamic force of cosmic dimension that can tackle and conquer super-king-sized problems. Your problems. The Bible says, "This is the victory that overcometh the world, even our faith." 1 John 5:4.

If we were not able to laugh at life's difficulties, they would soon prove too burdensome, and we would be buried under them. Our faith—our healthy, robust, positive outlook—helps us master these stressful situations before they master us. And as medical science has confirmed, faith is essential to our physical, mental, and spiritual well-being.

Dr. William S. Sadler, one of the founders of modern psychiatry, was so impressed by this profound relationship between faith and health that he wrote, "No one can appreciate so fully as a doctor the amazingly large percentage of human disease and suffering which is directly traceable to worry, fear, conflict, immorality, dissipation, and ignorance—to unwholesome thinking and unclean living. The simple acceptance of the principles and teachings of Christ with respect to the life of mental peace and joy, the life of unselfish thought and clean living, would at once wipe out more than half the difficulties, diseases, and sorrows of the human race. In other words, more than half of the present afflictions of mankind could be prevented by . . . living up to the personal and practical spirit of the real teachings of Christ. The teachings of Jesus applied to our modern civilization—understandingly applied, not merely nominally accepted—would so purify, uplift, and vitalize us that the race would immediately stand out as a new order of beings, possessing superior mental power and increased moral force. Irrespective of the future rewards of living, laying aside all discussion of future life, it would pay any man or woman to live the Christ-life just for the mental and moral rewards it affords here in this present world.''

Medical science attests to the rich dividends of Christian living. The faith of Jesus equips us to handle the hassles of everyday life. It is an invigorating force, a holy barrier against the attacks of the devil. The apostle Paul stated it this way: ''Put on all of God's armor so that you will be able to stand safe against all strategies and tricks of Satan.'' Ephesians 6:11, LB.

We might as well face the facts; stressful situations are a part of life. But in our faith we can ''overcome the world.'' We can face the future of this tension-filled world with confidence, for the future is in God's hands. His Spirit can help us maintain a wholesome and healthful attitude at all times—to have the ''mind of Christ.'' As Paul penned to the Philippians, ''Don't worry over anything whatever; . . . tell God every detail of your needs in thankful prayer, and the peace of God, which surpasses human understanding, will keep constant guard over your hearts and minds as they rest in Christ Jesus.'' Philippians 4:6, 7, Phillips.

CHAPTER 8
THE GOLDEN RULE

Whoever has the gold, makes the rules.

Economics. The thought of taking the class excited me about as much as the prospect of root-canal work. But my curriculum required that I take at least one accounting course, so I opted for Professor Moses Goldworm's class that met on Tuesday and Thursday afternoons in Reese Axelbank Hall.

As I perused the new fall bulletin, gleaning information about the course, I was amazed. I never fully realized the scope of economics. It suddenly hit me as if I had been struck with a wet mackerel—I was about to embark on a journey back in time to the very genesis epoch of human society. As I scanned the bulletin, my brain reeled around like a radar dish, overwhelmed by the immense bulk of knowledge before me. Imagine it! I was going to explore mankind's monetary origins. Talk about roots! Tears of joy blurred my vision as I read:

Economics I: In this course, the student will discover the backgrounds of our modern monetary system and learn why money is good. Much time is devoted to a discussion of coin versus currency, with an emphasis on obtaining currency since it takes less of it to purchase a new Frisbee. In addition, the student will learn about loans and credit (how to fill out an application), as well as inflation and depression, and how to dress for each. The course will also include an evaluation of checking and provide hints on how to keep a neat wallet. (Required reading: *The Art of Welshing.)*"

On Tuesday afternoon at two o'clock, I was in my place in the classroom, room #102, in Axelbank Hall. I neatly arranged my notebook, eraser, pencils, and pens, and awaited the arrival of Professor Goldworm.

In due time the hump-shouldered, graying, sometimes-cranky professor arrived, scanned the faces of the eager students, and mumbled something like, "And they call this education?"

We all chuckled lightly.

"Well, class," he began. "Welcome to economics. This is one of your favorite courses. I certainly hope it's one of mine."

Again muffled laughter.

"Economics. Don't let it scare you. Economics is really quite simple. It deals with the two great problems of life—how to make money and how to get along without it. You will discover that this course will prove invaluable to you as you embark on the great voyage of life, travel across the sea of time, through the hurricane of credit-card dependency, past the whirlpool of stocks, bonds, and time certificates, beyond the shoals of bankruptcy, to one day anchor safe in the harbor of financial security."

Everyone cheered. Remo Snarth made a sound like a fog horn.

"Whew, what a trip! I'll never make it into the harbor of security. I've already crashed on the shoals of bankruptcy," I said as I felt the plush lining of my empty pants pockets. My reverie was interrupted as the professor continued.

"Does this shock you?" said Professor Goldworm

5—B.K.L.

as he struck a match and set fire to a dollar bill.

Everyone in the class gasped.

"Aha!" said the professor with a satisfied gleam in his eye. "I see that it *does* shock you. And well it should. Because, you see, money is the stuff of life. Money is influence. Money is power. Money is clout. That's why the golden rule states: Whoever has the gold, makes the rules."

Again, chuckles and guffaws.

"Laugh if you will," said Professor Goldworm. "But sooner or later each of you must learn the value of a dollar. Even more important, you must learn that money talks. Money is the name of the game. The almighty greenback is *numero uno*. This is essentially what you will discover as you delve deeper into the complex world of economics."

We sat in petrified silence.

"Now, in preparation for our next class session, I would like each of you to study the first chapter in the textbook, entitled 'Monetary Origins.' This will bring your mind to focus on how our current system of checks and balances developed. It will take you back in time several millennia to ancient Mesopotamia—the cradle of human civilization. You will learn of the ancient Sumerians, who were instrumental in augmenting societal exchange practices. In this chapter you will undoubtedly encounter the name of Bildad of Ak. Born in the ancient city of Shu on the banks of the river Ulai, Bildad was the offspring of peasant parents—his father a serf, his mother a short-order cook at Fast Zillah's Gruel Take-Out. He it was who forged the very first coins and used these bronze metal disks in bartering for a used chariot. Prior to this time, such disks were used only for cuff links or for placing on the closed eyelids of the deceased. Disowned by his parents and ostracized from society, he set out for Egypt, where he spent three years in intensive research on papyrus as currency. He was so impressed with the prospect of paper money that he wrote: 'I am convinced that there is an enduring reality beyond our present consciousness—a juxtaposition of papyrus and green ink. Simplify. Simplify.' Yes, Bildad of Ak by his sheer creative genius was responsible for introducing coin and currency into the marketplace and, thus, forever altered the monetary landscape.''

I scribbled notes feverishly.

''Now, remember class, you will be accountable for all the material in the first chapter. We will have a quiz over this information at our next session. Class dismissed.''

We all filed out of the classroom and headed on to other appointments.

Later, in my dorm room in Newton Hall, I scanned the introductory chapter in the economics textbook. It was fascinating to learn about money and its origin and power. I realized that this one course of study would be invaluable to me in making a success of life.

But in the weeks and months that followed, I learned many other crucial lessons. Contrary to what Professor Goldworm had said, I discovered that money is *not* everything. It is not *numero uno*. Nor is it a panacea for all mankind's ills. Often money, or the love of money, is the root of many a perplexing problem. In fact, the apostle Paul stated in 1 Timothy 6:10 that ''the love of money is the root of all evil.''

Think of it! Love of money lies behind the staggering drug problem in our country today. Love of money is the reason for robbery, theft, and the soaring crime rate. Love of money is responsible for corruption in government and big business. Man's greed and selfishness have, more often than not, turned the blessing of riches into a terrible curse.

As if to attest to the universality of this evil, we have come to accept it cynically. Think of the sayings you have heard about money. For instance: "Money can't buy happiness, but it sure helps you look for it in a lot more places." Or, "Money can't buy everything—it can't buy poverty." Or, "Money may not be everything, but it's way ahead of whatever is in second place."

I'll be trite and declare the Christian view that money is *not* everything! Like everything else, the "almighty greenback" is doomed to oblivion. Only the things of God endure.

The emperor Charlemagne reigned for only fourteen years. But he sat on his throne for centuries. Charlemagne (Charles the Great) was crowned in the year 800 and ruled Western Europe until his death in 814. Then his body was dressed in imperial robes and a shining crown was placed on his head; on his finger was a signet ring, and a scepter, which symbolized power, was put in his hand. On his lap was placed a scroll listing noble deeds, victories in battle, and words of wisdom. The tomb, beneath the chapel Charlemagne had built at his capital city of Aix-la-Chapelle in Prussia, was sealed—never to be opened. But in the year 1001, by order of Emperor Otho III, the seal was broken and the tomb opened. What greeted the eyes of the excavators was an eerie sight. There sat a skeleton upon a throne inlaid with precious stones. At his feet was a heap of dust which had once been flesh and kingly robes. The beautiful crown had dropped to his shoulders and the signet ring lay a shining circlet on the stony floor. Time had eaten away the hand that grasped the scepter, and as it fell beside the ring, the scroll on his lap had unrolled and the bony finger rested upon the parchment, pointing to the words: "What shall it profit a man, if he gain the whole world, and lose his own soul?" Mark 8:36.

Riches, wealth are fleeting. And the person who places his hope and confidence in money and material things will ultimately be disappointed.

The wise man, Solomon, said it centuries ago, "There is that maketh himself rich, yet hath nothing: there is that maketh himself poor, yet hath great riches." Proverbs 13:7.

I submit that a life of unselfish service to God and others more nearly reaches the standard of heaven than the life of any selfish millionaire. The highest attribute of man is not to get something for nothing, but rather to give something for nothing. The truly wealthy man or woman is one whose fortune is spiritual, not temporal.

It is recorded that Jesus once said to His disciples, "Lay not up for yourselves treasures upon earth, . . . but lay up for yourselves treasure in heaven." Mathew 6:19, 20.

How do you make deposits in heaven's bank—New Jerusalem's First Savings and Trust? I contend that we lay up treasure by giving oneself and one's means in service to God and to man. This means that you will look for opportunities to serve.

You will support your church in its witnessing outreach, no matter how inconvenient it is for you. You will not just believe it is right to be a Good Samaritan, you will be one. You will not merely agree in principle that everything you have belongs to God, but you will actually render an honest tithe. You will not insist on being first in line at every church potluck, nor will you be last to show up when they have a church work bee.

You will not ponder how much you have, but rather what you can give in service to others.

"Whoever has the gold, makes the rules" may seem to be true in this life. But in the sight of heaven, the life of Christian service is the only life that will reap dividends.

CHAPTER 9
LYNCH'S LAW

When the going gets tough, everyone leaves.

Chem lab was the pits! I had better things to do with my Thursday afternoons than to fool around with beakers, flasks, pipettes, and assorted chemicals. Talk about dullsville! This was it! However, I realized all too well that if I was going to graduate in the spring, I would have to rough it out. Chem lab was the only major obstacle between me and a diploma. I figured I could handle it.

This particular Thursday afternoon, I was one of three guys who had yet to complete the lab assignment. As fate would have it, the trio consisted of Clovis Shonkwiler, Elmo Wartman, and me.

Now Clovis and Elmo were my good friends, but I have to be honest—they were not overly bright. In fact, I would estimate their combined IQ to be no more than 67 max! This shortage of mental acumen coupled with a hefty dose of dumbness on my part would soon yield some volatile results.

"Hey, Big K, how is your experiment going?" asked Clovis as he peered at me from the opposite side of the lab counter.

"OK, I guess. I still have to add some sodium chloride to this solution of acid and see if it reacts."

"Hang it up, man!" Elmo wailed. "The whole experiment is a bummer! All it does is fizz for a few seconds and it's over, kaput, done!''

I carefully poured the sodium chloride crystals into the beaker of solution and waited. There was a momentary reaction—bubbling and fizzing—and that was all. Hmmmm!

"See! What did I tell you!" said Elmo as he walked over and observed the lifeless liquid. "We work our fingers to the bone for over an hour combining this chemical with that chemical, this solution with that solution, and for what? A fleeting fizz! I tell you, Keith, it's a downright disgrace!''

"Yeah!" chimed in Clovis. "I paid good money for this course, and I expect more than a feeble fizz!"

"I understand how you two feel," I said, trying to add a note of sanity to the discussion. "But the reason we are practicing simple experiments now is to learn the rudimentary techniques of chemistry. We are not capable of handling dangerous, explosive substances. Something could go wrong.''

"Hogwash!" huffed Elmo. "We are three reasonably intelligent young men. There isn't anything we couldn't handle. Besides, I'm bored to death of these Mickey Mouse experiments. All these tests have been done a million times and with the same results. Why don't we try a real experiment—something totally different?''

Clovis nodded in agreement.

"Now wait a minute," I said. "You guys have got to be kidding. We could get in a lot of trouble.''

"Nonsense!" laughed Elmo. "Professor Yollberry won't be back for at least an hour. We've got it made in the shade! Relax, Big K, you're going to enjoy this.''

"What experiment did you two have in mind?" I asked tentatively.

"Clovis read about it in *Science Digest*," said Elmo. "You're going to get a charge out of this one." Elmo prodded Clovis in the ribs, and they both laughed.

"Are you two sure you know what you're doing?"

"Hey," responded Clovis. "Did Edison know what he was doing when he invented the telphone? Of course we know what we're doing!"

I shook my head.

"Go into the supply room, Clovis, and get some potassium permanganate and glycerin," said Elmo. "And hurry. This is going to be great!" Elmo rubbed his hands together.

In a minute, Clovis returned clutching the precious substances.

"Now, Big K, place the large beaker in the metal holder and tighten the clamp." Elmo commanded.

Reluctantly I obeyed.

"Clovis, pour the potassium permanganate into the beaker. Don't be stingy; empty the whole thing in there. We want this to be good."

Clovis followed instructions until not a speck of the dark colored powder was left in the can.

"All right," said Elmo with a note of finality in his voice. "Now, for the finishing touch." And with that he dumped a healthy helping of glycerin into the powder-filled beaker.

We all scrambled for cover, cowering behind the counter, waiting to see what would happen.

Nothing. Nothing at all. Not even a fizz.

"What a disappointment," lamented Elmo. My friends' faces registered their dejection.

"Big deal! Some great experiment!" I chided them as the three of us stood to our feet and walked toward the dormant container.

Suddenly, like a surrealistic vision from some horrific view of the end of the world, it happened. ARMA-GEDDON! WHOOSH! A huge jet of fire shot upward to the ceiling. KABOOM! The beaker discharged like a cannon volley and shattered in a million pieces. POP! PING! KAPOW! Flasks, pipettes, and beakers were exploding all around us as ignited projectiles screamed about the room. Clovis, Elmo, and I hit the floor and covered our heads anticipating death. The lab was choked with noxious fumes and billowing smoke.

"Let's get out of here!" I hollered, as we crawled toward the door.

Once outside we coughed and sputtered and tried to catch our breath.

"Wow! Was that a trip!" said Elmo, swallowing hard.

"I can't believe it!" cried Clovis. "We must have used too much gunpowder."

"Gunpowder!" I yelled. "You mean to tell me that stuff—potassium permanganate—was actually gunpowder?"

Elmo and Clovis grinned sheepishly.

"Are you two out of your gourds! You nitwits could have gotten us killed! We could have demolished the entire school!"

When things had calmed down in the lab, we went back inside to open the windows, air out the room, and survey the damage. We couldn't believe what had happened. In stunned silence we stared at the devastation.

The huge jet of fire had shot upward, melting the fluorescent light fixture and blackening the ceiling. The metal apparatus used to hold the beaker had fused into a molten mass and had seared through the counter top to the floor below. And the room was strewn with broken glass and bits of debris. In total, it looked like a war zone.

"I hope you two are satisfied," I said in disgust and turned my back to them.

"Hey, Big K, that's real bad what happened to your equipment there," consoled Elmo.

"What do you mean?" I asked warily.

"You know, me and Clovis are sorry that your experiment caused all that damage."

"*My* experiment!" I thundered. "What are you talking about? This whole thing was *your* idea. You guys aren't going to wiggle out of this one."

"Listen, Big K," said Elmo as he put his arm around my shoulder. "Clovis and me would like nothing better than to stay until Professor Yollbery returns, but unfortunately we have a previous commitment."

"Commitment. What commitment?" I said skeptically.

"Clovis and me—ah we have to shampoo the carpets in our dorm room. Right, Clovis?"

"Right!" chimed Clovis. "See you around, Big K."

"Hey, wait! You two dimwits get back here this very minute! I mean it! I'm not kidding!" All the while I hollered, they ran pell mell back to the dorm.

And when Professor Yollberry returned to the lab a few minutes later, guess who was the only one around to explain what had happened to his war-torn classroom. That's right. Me.

I cite this woeful tale to prove a point. Lynch's law states: "When the going gets tough, everyone leaves." The stern dicta of life demonstrates the veracity of Lynch's pronouncement. Who knows, maybe he even knew Elmo and Clovis!

In any case, it seems that when the going gets roughest, some of our "tried and true friends" have a way of vanishing into the proverbial woodwork. Right? I learned this lesson the hard way.

75

In the complex and dangerous field of international espionage, they have a rule which is strictly practiced by every nation. The dogma is simply stated. It is called the "doctrine of deniability." This doctrine has far-reaching implications to every person involved in the spy game.

It means that if you are ever caught by the enemy in an act of espionage, your country will categorically disavow any knowledge of you and your actions. In short, they will deny they know you. Even the government of the United States has invoked this doctrine on numerous occasions and has left spies and agents to the mercy of hostile, foreign nations.

Peter was a loyal follower of Jesus. He boasted that he would never turn his back on the Saviour. Until one dark night outside a judgment hall, he succumbed to external pressure and denied that he knew the Saviour. Not once, but three times.

Maybe there have been times in your own experience, when you—by your words and actions—denied that you were a friend of Jesus. You yielded to the pressure of the moment and turned your back on the Saviour.

I'm glad that God doesn't practice the "doctrine of deniability" with us. Instead, when things get the roughest, He is always there. When there's a storm on the lake, He comes to the rescue across the water. When alone and fearful we huddle in the upper room, He comes bringing comfort and confidence. When we are heartbroken because of our failures, like Peter was, He soothes the hurt with a hug. And says, "Everyone else may deny you, but I'll never deny you. But I'll confess your name to my Father and to His angels." See Revelation 3:5.

Clovis and Elmo left me holding the bag. Peter rejected his Lord. You may have discredited Him too. Don't be afraid. He will never deny you. But rather He says, "I will never leave you; I will never abandon you." Hebrews 13:5, TEV. When the going gets tough —*He's there!*

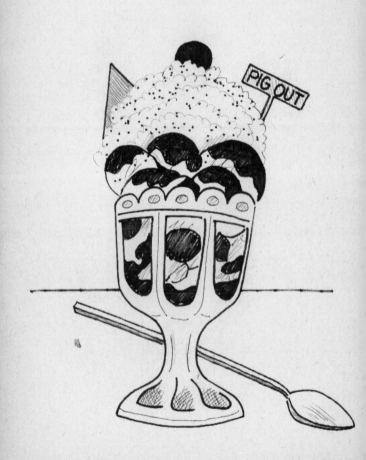

CHAPTER 10
CLAIRVAUX'S CODICIL

The things we love, we grow to resemble.

M was fat—disgustingly fat! (His real name is Eulas Quattlebaum, but to protect him from embarrassment, we shall call him M.) M was the fattest human I have ever known. Excess poundage protruded all over his body. Fat dripped off of him like fudge dripping off a hot fudge sundae. His fingers were fat. His ankles were fat. His eyes were fat. (Can you imagine fat eyes?) His girth was beyond belief. Nothing remotely resembling M exists today—save perhaps in the annals of science fiction. I mean this guy was Lard City. A crime against nature.

Now, you may ask: Is this a gross exaggeration of fact? Nay. Nix. Negatory. M was as obese as this statement implies—only more so. He was porcine to such a degree that he could not fit through the average doorframe without a hydraulic assist. And thus, M was no stranger to insults hurled at him by gangs of young rowdies. Frequently he was stung by cries of "Tubby" and "Blimpo." Particularly cruel was one occasion when an elderly woman called out, "Hey, Tiny, why don't you get your own zip code?" Heartless.

No one knew how much M weighed or whether he had ever seen his feet. (Rumor had it that he had last glimpsed them in the spring of 1962.) Everyone did

know, however, that not only was M fat, but he was
also a slob. He was positively gross. He is the only person I've ever known that trimmed his nose hairs with a
Weed-Eater. He clad his bulging torso in the grossest,
gaudiest threads. His red and yellow, broad-checked,
double-knit slacks looked like clown pants straight out
of circus world. His shirts always bore huge food
stains. His black-horn-rimmed glasses were as thick as
coke bottle bottoms. And his once-white athletic socks
and scuffed brown shoes made him the laughingstock
of the college campus.

M's favorite hideout on campus was (as you might
have guessed) the Snak Shop. At almost any hour of
the day or night, you could find M overflowing a booth,
stuffing his ballooning face.

He loved to dine on the so-called Pig-Out Delight, a
super sundae intended to satisfy eight to ten. As the
menu explains, the Pig-Out Delight consists of a mountain of ice cream (5 scoops of vanilla, 5 scoops of
chocolate, 5 scoops of strawberry), overlayed with
gobs of fudge, caramel, and marshmallow topping,
frothy mounds of whipped cream, assorted nuts, sprin-
kles, and a maraschino cherry imported from Ojai. It's
enough to make you barf. However, M downed the Delight with amazing regularity. Unreal!

Then M met O. (Her real name is Opadell Webley,
but I do this purely to avoid a costly lawsuit.)

Now, O was not exactly a "prize catch," if you get
my drift. But she had worlds more class than M. True,
she was a bit stout, but compared to M, she was a
Twiggy.

Suddenly, M and O fell madly in love. And overnight
they became a campus "item." They were seen together at every collegiate event—the Moonlight Mean-
der, the Reverse-Date Banquet, the Lyceums. They

were inseparable. Like Tarzan and Jane, Bonnie and Clyde, peaches and cream.

And amazingly M began to change. Oh, at first the alterations were subtle. But gradually a metamorphosis took place. He began to comb his hair and brush his teeth. It was evident that M was taking a real interest in himself. He even began to shrink, necessitating the purchase of some new threads to replace his gross, grubby garments.

Word had it that he had joined Weight Watchers. Someone even said that he attended regular workout sessions at "Jimmy Joe Redsky's Fat Cat Health Spa and Weight Loss Emporium" in Calistoga.

Well, something was obviously happening, because in a few short months a transformation was wrought. No doubt, you have seen these "before" and "after" shots in magazines, where an obese woman in Ladlespoon, North Carolina, lost 125 pounds of ugly fat in just two weeks. These ads are almost too much to be believed. And yet with M it was true! His portly frame was whittled down to size in no time. It was M in the flesh (or the lack of it) down to a svelte 186 pounds. He looked smashing in his new Johnny Carson suit, Pierre Cardin tie, and Gucci shoes. Incredible!

"Eulas, is that you?" I ventured, as I saw him standing in the lobby of the dorm.

"Yep," he beamed.

"Man, you look great! What happened?"

He looked at me with a grin and answered in one word, "Love."

I got the message.

In the months that followed, not only did Eulas and Opadell grow to love one another. They grew alike. Same laugh. Same likes and dislikes. Same idiosyncrasies. They even began to look like each other. Scary.

6—B.K.L.

But not really, for what happened with Eulas and Opadell is a simple law of life.

Clairvaux's Codicil states: "The things we love, we grow to resemble." In making this pronouncement, the ancient churchman, Bernard of Clairvaux, was enunciating psychological and spiritual principles with far-reaching ramifications.

In the book *The Great Controversy*, page 555, Ellen White comments on this aspect of Christian living. "It is a law both of the intellectual and the spiritual nature that by beholding we become changed. The mind gradually adapts itself to the subjects upon which it is allowed to dwell. It becomes assimilated to that which it is accustomed to love and reverence."

How does this work? It happens because of the marvelous way the mind is constituted. The mind is an amazing and delicate instrument.

Your brain is about three pounds of pinkish-gray mass not much larger than a softball. As you read the words on this page, tiny electric shocks are stimulating the cells of your mind into restless action. Sensory impressions stream into your brain at the rate of several billion per second. To duplicate its action would take a computer larger than the Empire State Building. Several lifetimes would be required just to wire it. Its electric power requirements would demand much of the supply of all the hydroelectric dams on the Columbia River, and the river itself would have to be diverted to cool the computer.

Massachusetts Institute of Technology scientists have estimated that during a person's lifetime it is possible to store about forty times as much information as is contained in the nearly fifteen million volumes in the Library of Congress. And yet all this is neatly packed between your two ears.

You see, to put it simply, in the human mind are two distinct mechnisms: The instinctive memory and the reasoning mind. The instinctive memory we might liken to a cassette recorder. The reasoning mind acts much like a computer. These two mechanisms operate as independently as do your hands from your feet.

Your five senses report to your instinctive memory. For there is recorded the raw data from which quick decisions are made. You apply the brake on your car to avoid another vehicle almost automatically. The instinctive memory must react now, instantly to survive.

The reasoning mind must consider and calculate different possibilities—a much slower process.

The instinctive memory—like a cassette recorder—cannot think. It simply records and plays back information. It is like the file drawer of the subconscious. And deep within the file drawer is the raw data from which we make judgments and take action.

In the tissues of your mind, writes Gilbert Highet in *Man's Unconquerable Mind*, are "recorded and stored billions upon billions of memories, habits, instincts, desires and hopes and fears and patterns and tinctures and sounds and inconceivably delicate calculations and brutishly crude urgencies, the sound of a whisper heard thirty years ago, . . . the delight never experienced but incessantly imagined, the complex structure of stresses in a bridge, the exact pressure of a single finger on a single string, the development of ten thousand different games of chess, the precise curve of a lip, a hill, an equation or a flying ball, tones and shades, and glooms and raptures, the faces of countless strangers, the scent of one garden, inventions, poems, jokes, tunes, sums, problems unsolved, victories long past, the fear of hell and the love of God, the vision of a blade of grass and and a sky filled with stars.

This is the function of the instinctive memory. And recordings that are repeated over and over become habits or automatic reactions. These habits or automatic reactions can even overcome the reasoning mind.

Hence we can become addicted to various things—drugs, alcohol, sugar, TV. Gradually the mind adapts itself to that upon which it is allowed to dwell. "The things we love, we grow to resemble."

Never more true words were spoken than those of the wise man, Solomon, recorded in the book of Proverbs. "As [a man] thinketh in his heart, so is he." Proverbs 23:7.

What commands your attention? What do you dwell upon or think about? What do you love?

If we constantly expose our minds to worldly influences the result is that we will become like the world. If we dwell on movies or TV shows that highlight violence, infidelity, promiscuity, and the nonvalues of our culture, that is exactly what we will become. If our music and literature is saturated with immoral themes and blatant degeneracy, what can we expect? Words of wisdom from an ancient sage drum against our conscience: "But we all . . . beholding . . . are changed." 2 Corinthians 3:18.

Dr. William James, who was professor of physiology and, later, philosophy at Harvard and who published *Principles of Psychology* in 1876, explained what this means: "The hell to be endured hereafter, of which theology tells, is no worse than the hell we make for ourselves in this world by habitually fashioning our characters in the wrong way. Could the young but realize how soon they will become mere walking bundles of habits, they would give more heed to their conduct while in the plastic state. We are spinning our own fates, good or evil, and never to be undone. Every smallest stroke of virtue or of vice leaves its never so little scar. The drunken Rip Van Winkle, in Jefferson's play, excuses himself for every fresh dereliction by saying, 'I won't count this time!' Well, he may not count it, and a kind Heaven may not count it; but it is being counted nonetheless. Down among his nerve-cells and fibers the molecules are counting it, registering and storing it up to be used against him when the next temptation comes. Nothing we ever do is in the strict scientific literalness, wiped out."

The witness of the Bible, the evidence of science, the testimony of our sense, all support the conclusion: Everything that crosses the threshold of the mind changes us. "The things we love, we grow to resemble."

What happened to Eulas and Opadell was a direct result of this basic law of life. How important it is to fill our minds with positive values. To read good books. Listen to good music. To view uplifting television programs. Surround ourselves with friends whose conversation and values reflect spirituality. Model our conduct after what would be pleasing to God.

As the apostle Paul declared, "And the peace of God, which passeth all understanding, shall keep our hearts and minds through Christ Jesus. Finally, brethren, whatsoever things are true, whatsoever things are honest, whatsoever things are just, whatsoever things are pure, whatsoever things are lovely, whatsoever things are of good report; if there be any virtue, and if there be any praise, think on these things." Philippians 4:7, 8.

MATZ'S MAXIM: A conclusion is the place where you got tired of thinking.

HETZBERG'S FIRST LAW OF WING WALKING: Never leave hold of what you've got until you've got hold of something else.

KNOCHE'S OBSERVATION: A foot is a device for finding furniture in the dark.

BARTH'S DISTINCTION: There are two types of people: those who divide people into two types, and those who do not.

SATTINGER'S LAW: It works better if you plug it in.

CHAPTER 11
THE LAW OF
COMMONALITY

Always remember that you are absolutely unique—just like everyone else.

The announcement on the poster read: COSTUME PARTY, SPONSORED BY TAU BETA EPSILON, SATURDAY NIGHT AT 8:00, TONGA ROOM, SANTA ROSA, FOOD AND FUN, PRIZES AWARDED FOR BEST COSTUME, BEST COUPLE, MOST ORIGINAL COSTUME.

I was looking forward to the costume party. After all, I was escorting lovely and vivacious Sarah Bellum to the festive event. It was being sponsored by the Girls' Club—Tau Beta Epsilon—and was to be held in the Tonga Room, high atop the fabulous Astro Car Wash in beautiful downtown Santa Rosa (pop. 50,000). Too much!

Sarah and I discussed our costumes as we munched our breakfast granola in the cafeteria.

"I'm going as Little Bo Peep," she gushed. "Keith, you'll just love my outfit. It's darling. My aunt Thelma is sewing the whole thing by hand. I have a cute bonnet and a real staff and everything! Oooh, I'm so excited!" she squealed.

"Yeah!" I mumbled with an obvious lack of enthusiasm.

"Tell me, Keith," she cooed. "Who are you going as?"

"I don't know. I haven't decided."

"How about going as Count Dracula?" Sarah ventured, her eyes dancing.

"Naw! Too common. I have my eye on the prize for most original costume."

"Well, there's always Robin Hood or Julius Caesar."

"Sarah, everybody will be dressed like Robin Hood or Julius Caesar."

"I've got it!" she snapped her little fingers. "You go as Charlie Chaplin—the Little Tramp!"

"Earth to Sarah. Earth to Sarah," I said in monotone. "Come in, Sarah. You're not reading me."

Sarah didn't seem amused.

"Look," I continued. "I don't want to be someone average or run-of-the-mill. I want to be someone unusual, rare, totally uncommon. I want a character and costume that demonstrate my imagination, creativity, my own persona. It has to be a special identity that reflects my uniqueness as an individual, not just a carbon copy of someone else. Do you understand?"

"I guess so," she replied meekly. "I just wish you'd go as Charlie Chaplin."

"Never! But don't fear. I'll come up with the perfect personality and costume by Saturday night. You'll see. Bye."

Back in my dorm room, I paced back and forth. I had to come up with the ideal character for the party. Monumental giants of history, art, science, literature, stage, and screen loomed in my mind—Raphael, Amenhotep IV, Mahatma Gandhi, Mad King Ludwig of Bavaria, Burt Convey, Babe Ruth. . . .

After nearly an hour of contemplation, it suddenly hit me. My eyes accidentally fell upon my open biology textbook. The name literally leaped out at me—Gregor

Mendel. Sure, why not! I would go to the costume party as Gregor Mendel, Austrian monk and geneticist. Perfect!

I ran to the library and searched out an ancient, dust-covered volume which contained a crude woodcut of the renowned scientist in his native garb. The caption read: Mendel at Lornstatz on the Rhine.

"Perfect!" I reiterated. "I can get most of the outfit from the costume rental store in Berkeley, a beard from the drama department, a capuche and tunic from my old friend, Reginald Fishbein, and leggings and brogues from here and there. Oh, boy, this is going to be great!" I exulted, rubbing my hands together.

On the evening of the party, I donned my beard, vestments, tunic, capuche, et cetera. As I inspected myself in the mirror, it was almost scary. I was the flawless embodiment of Gregor Mendel. It was as if the master geneticist were walking the earth again.

I picked up Bo Peep (Sarah Bellum) at the girls' dorm, and we drove to Santa Rosa in my VW. I parked the car outside the Astro Car Wash, and the two of us walked to the entrance.

"I still don't understand who you're supposed to be," said Sarah in exasperation. "Are you Groucho Marx or what?"

"Just trust me, Sarah," I assured her. "I'm going to win the prize this evening for most unusual costume, simply because my outfit is different. I am L. Unique!"

As we walked in the door of the Tonga Room, I was greeted by Warren Friedman, dressed in beard, vestments, tunic, and capuche. "Nice Gregor Mendel outfit you've got there, Keith," he said blandly. "Isn't it remarkable that we came as the same person?"

I was dumbfounded. "Impossible!" I thought.

But as I looked over the room, I became more

distraught. There was Tom Ironwelder as Gregor Mendel, as well as Boaz Schwump as the famous geneticist. Before my swimming eyes Mendels were coming out of the woodwork.

"I—I—I—think I'd better sit down," I stammered to Sarah. "I don't feel so good."

"I'll go get you some punch," she said, and disappeared.

"I must be in the Twilight Zone," I thought to myself. "Or else I'm on Candid Camera. Maybe this is a Gregor Mendel Look-Alike Contest!"

"Hiya, Keith!" I turned to see Amanda Philpott standing there in—you guessed it—beard, vestments, tunic, and capuche.

"Let me guess. You're Gregor Mendel, right?" I droned.

"Right!" she laughed. "Isn't it strange that we came to the party as the same person. What are the chances of that happening, do you suppose?"

I grimaced.

"Oh, by the way," Amanda continued, "I like the feather in your hat. Nice touch. Wish I had thought of that."

I shrugged and she walked away.

"Here, drink some of this." It was Sarah, holding out a glass of potable potion. "It'll make you feel better."

She sat down beside me as I gulped down the red liquid.

"I just don't understand it," I lamented. "I was sure nobody would come dressed as Gregor Mendel. And as it turned out, everybody came dressed as Gregor Mendel—even Amanda! That really burns my cookies!"

"There, there," consoled Sarah. "Relax and enjoy

yourself. So you may not win the prize for the most original outfit. So what! Who knows; maybe I'll win. I'm the only Bo Peep."

I grimaced again.

Now I don't think Sarah's a prophet, but her words seemed strangely prophetic. And by evening's end they were to become truth. For when the prizes were awarded, she carted home the trophy engraved "Most Original Costume." Can you believe it?

Why do I cite this obviously painful story? To prove a valuable point. The Law of Commonality states: "Always remember that you are absolutely unique—just like everyone else."

You may feel that you are different from everyone else, but in God's eyes we are all the same. That does not mean that we are all Xeroxed duplicates of each other. No. But it does mean that we are all transgressors of His law.

The Living Bible puts it this way in Romans 3:23, "Yes, all have sinned; all fall short of God's glorious ideal." The Scriptures confirm our guilty status and further pronounce a death penalty on every human being. "The wages of sin is death." Romans 6:23.

The Bible teaches that every person born into this world has a common denominator—we are all sinners destined to die. This commonality knows no station or rank.

Charles DeGaulle and Robert Ingersol, John Milton and Conrad Hilton, Carol Burnett and Anwar Sadat, Elvis Presley and John Wesley, Charlemagne and King Hussein, Dolly Parton and Billy Martin, Jimmy Hoffa and Neil Sedaka, Mao Tse Tung and Rev. Moon, Lucille Ball and Pope John Paul II, Golda Meier and Sonny and Cher, Jackie O. and Fidel Castro, Jim Fixx and Richard Nixon, Ralph Nader and Truman Capote,

Willie Mays and Rutherford B. Hayes, John Wayne and Thomas Paine, Uri Geller and John Davison Rockefeller, Ronald Reagan and Menachem Begin, Marilyn Monroe and Vincent Van Gogh, Dustin Hoffman and Andy Kaufman, Laurel and Hardy, and Vince Lombardi and Mary Tyler Moore. We all need Jesus, sooner or later. His love is a common denominator. We are all sinners needing His grace, or we'll each die alone, lost in space.

Peter was right when he said, in Acts 10:34, that ''God is no respecter of persons.'' But we can be thankful that God's free grace is available to everyone!